IF YOU WERE A KID ON THE
Oregon Trail

BY JOSH GREGORY · ILLUSTRATED BY LLUÍS FARRÉ

CHILDREN'S PRESS®

An Imprint of Scholastic Inc.

Content Consultant
James Marten, PhD, Professor and Chair, History Department, Marquette University

Photo credits ©: 9: Sueddeutsche Zeitung Photo/Alamy Images; 11: Apic/Getty Images; 13: Pictorial Pres Ltd/Alamy Images; 15: Chuck Franklin/Alamy Images; 17: Nebraska State Historical Society (RG0953-AM-8-9); 19: Nancy Carter/North Wind Picture Archives; 21: Sergei Drozd/Shutterstock, Inc.; 23: The New York Historical Society/Getty Images; 25: Peteforsyth/Wikimedia; 26: Columbia Gorge Discovery Center & Museum; 29: Yulia Glam/Shutterstock, Inc.

Library of Congress Cataloging-in-Publication Data
Names: Gregory, Josh, author. | Farré, Lluís, 1970- illustrator.
Title: If you were a kid on the Oregon Trail / by Josh Gregory ; Illustrated by Lluís Farré.
Other titles: On the Oregon Trail
Description: New York : Children's Press, an Imprint of Scholastic Inc., 2016. | Series: If you were a kid | Includes bibliographical references and index.
Identifiers: LCCN 2015043534| ISBN 9780531219706 (library binding : alk. paper) | ISBN 9780531221679 (pbk. : alk. paper)
Subjects: LCSH: Oregon Territory—History—Juvenile literature. | Overland journeys to the Pacific—Juvenile literature. | Frontier and pioneer life—West (U.S.)—Juvenile literature. | West (U.S.)—History—19th century—Juvenile literature.
Classification: LCC F597 .G795 2016 | DDC 978—dc23
LC record available at http://lccn.loc.gov/2015043534

2 3 4 5 6 7 **8** 9 10 R 26 25 24 23 22 21 20 19 **18** 17

TABLE OF CONTENTS

A Different Way of Life

During the mid-19th century, many people left their homes and traveled westward to Oregon in search of a better life. Most of them followed a path we know today as the Oregon Trail. Imagine you were a kid traveling on the trail. The clothes you wear, the kind of home you live in, and the foods you eat would be different. You wouldn't go to school. Instead, you would walk for hours and hours every day. You would cross dusty plains, green forests, and steep mountains on foot. It would be a difficult journey and, even after arriving, life wouldn't always be easy. Despite all this, around the 1850s many people traveled thousands of miles to cross the country in search of a new place to call home.

Turn the page to set off on your own journey west! You will see that life today is a lot different than it was in the past.

Meet Stephen!

This is Stephen Byrd. It is spring of 1845, and he and his family have left their home in Pennsylvania. They are heading to Oregon, where there is land available for them to start a farm. Though Stephen is excited about the trip, he is sad that he has to leave his friends and relatives behind. Stephen's mom tells him that he will make plenty of new friends out west. However, he is still worried that he will be lonely in Oregon . . .

Meet Josephine!

This is Josephine Jenkins. Two years ago, her father left the family behind in St. Louis, Missouri, and traveled to Oregon. There, he opened a shop to sell supplies to other **emigrants**. It was a great success, and now Josephine is traveling with her mother and younger brothers to join him. She is excited to see her father again. She is also looking forward to seeing the West. Though she has never left St. Louis before, she has an adventurous spirit. She can't wait to write about the trip in her journal . . .

It was a bright, sunny morning in May 1845. The town of Independence, Missouri, was full of activity. A huge crowd gathered there each spring to begin their journey on the Oregon Trail. Stephen and Josephine were among the many people finishing preparations for the trip. Stephen helped his dad make sure their wagon was ready. Josephine and her mom packed their family's many supplies.

STAYING IN TOUCH

If you moved across the country today, it would be easy to stay in touch with old friends. You could call on the phone anytime you liked. You might even video chat or text. But none of this was possible in the days of the Oregon Trail. Back then, it was difficult to even send a paper letter back home. There was no mail service yet!

Traveling the Oregon Trail made it hard to stay in touch with family and friends.

Soon, a few wagons at a time, everyone began setting off on the trail. It was the beginning of a very long journey. Traveling the entire 2,000 miles (3,218 kilometers) of the Oregon Trail would take them between five and six months.

Near the front of the group, Stephen rode on horseback alongside his father. Farther back, Josephine walked next to her family's wagon with her younger brothers.

A VERY LONG TRIP

Today, it is much easier to travel from Missouri to Oregon. Traveling by car on modern roads, it takes less than 24 hours. By airplane, it takes just under four hours. People did not have these options during the time of westward expansion. Instead, they walked or rode horses.

They crossed what are now the states of Kansas, Nebraska, Wyoming, and Idaho. There were no roads, and the **terrain** was difficult and even dangerous in places.

A group of settlers heading west sometime around 1850

By evening, everyone was very tired. All the wagons stopped in a big group. Some people began cooking dinner. Others made sure the animals had food and water.

Josephine was excited to write about the day in her journal. She had seen many exciting things. But as she searched the wagon, she started to panic.

"Oh no!" she cried.

"My journal is gone!"

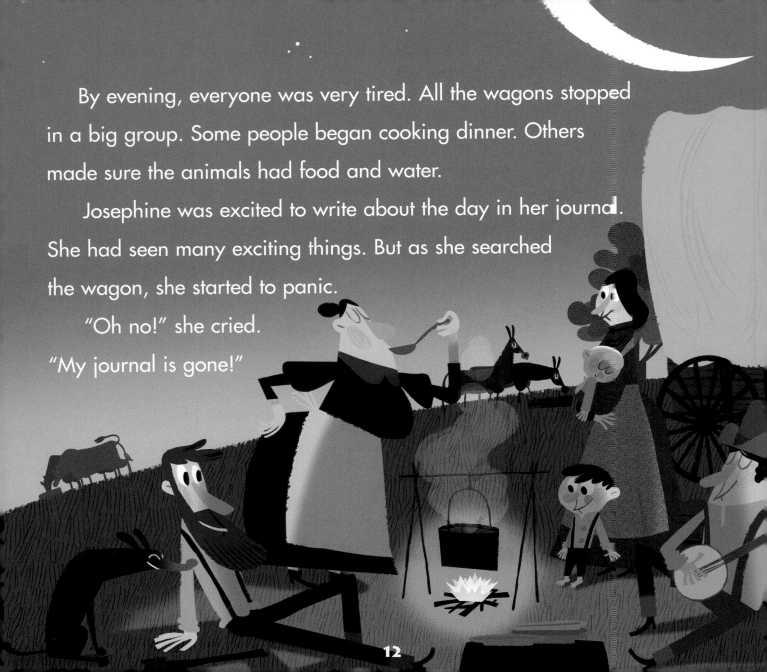

NIGHTS UNDER THE STARS

If you were traveling across the country today, you would probably stop at a hotel to sleep. But there were no hotels during the time of the Oregon Trail. Each night, people camped outside in the wilderness. They ate simple food such as beans, rice, and bacon. They built fires to stay warm and slept on the ground. Some of the men took turns sleeping so they could watch out for wild animals and other dangers.

A group of settlers takes a break from their westward journey sometime around 1850.

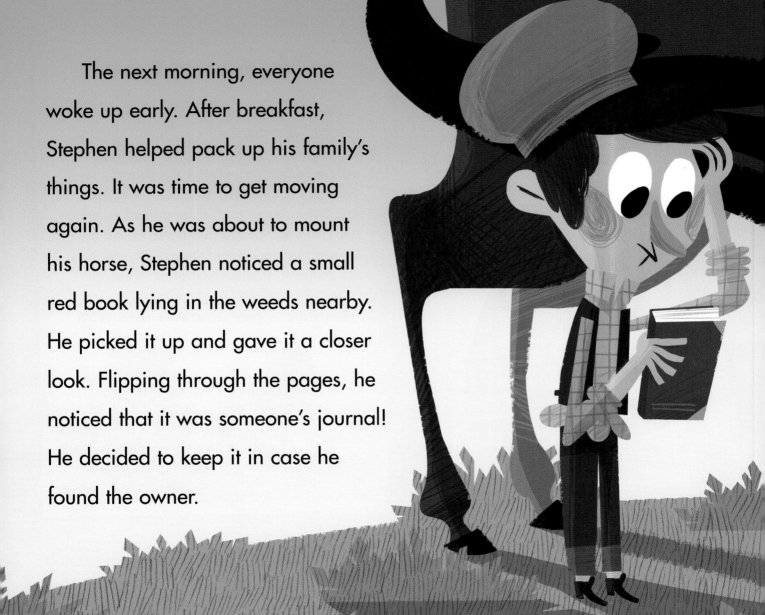

The next morning, everyone woke up early. After breakfast, Stephen helped pack up his family's things. It was time to get moving again. As he was about to mount his horse, Stephen noticed a small red book lying in the weeds nearby. He picked it up and gave it a closer look. Flipping through the pages, he noticed that it was someone's journal! He decided to keep it in case he found the owner.

KIDS' DAILY CHORES

There wasn't much time to play or relax while traveling on the Oregon Trail. Children were expected to help out with many chores. Some cared for younger brothers and sisters. Others collected water. This helped save time for the adults to do other important jobs.

Buckets were used to collect water from streams and other nearby sources.

Every day continued much the same way. The group woke up early, traveled all day, and camped at night. Along the way, Josephine was amazed at the incredible sights. The group crossed **vast** plains and climbed hills so high she could see for miles. They even passed a huge rock shaped like a chimney! Josephine wished she could describe the amazing views in her journal.

RECORDING THE JOURNEY

If you went on a trip today, you would probably take photos along the way. Oregon Trail travelers didn't have this opportunity. Though the earliest cameras had been invented, they were rare and difficult to use. Instead, most people recorded the things they saw by drawing pictures and keeping notes. Many of them carried journals.

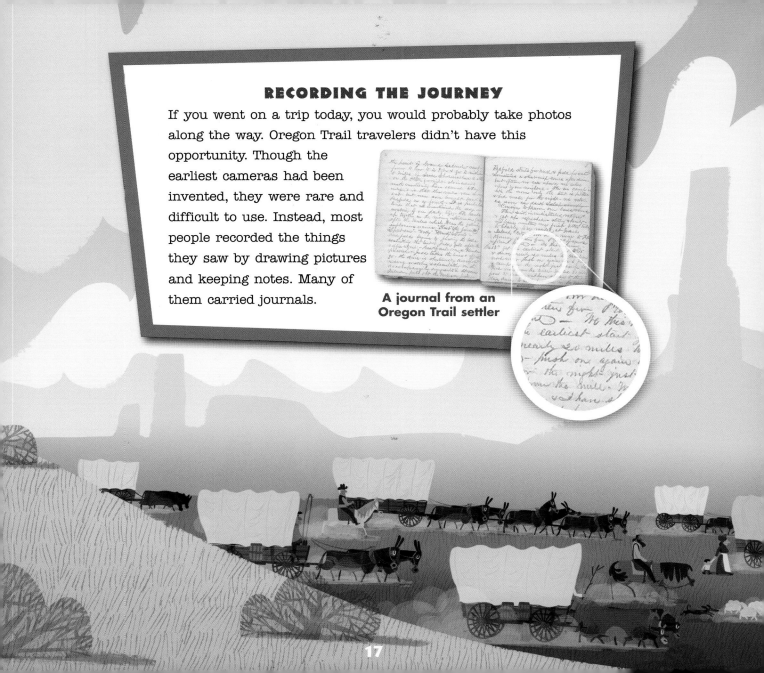

A journal from an Oregon Trail settler

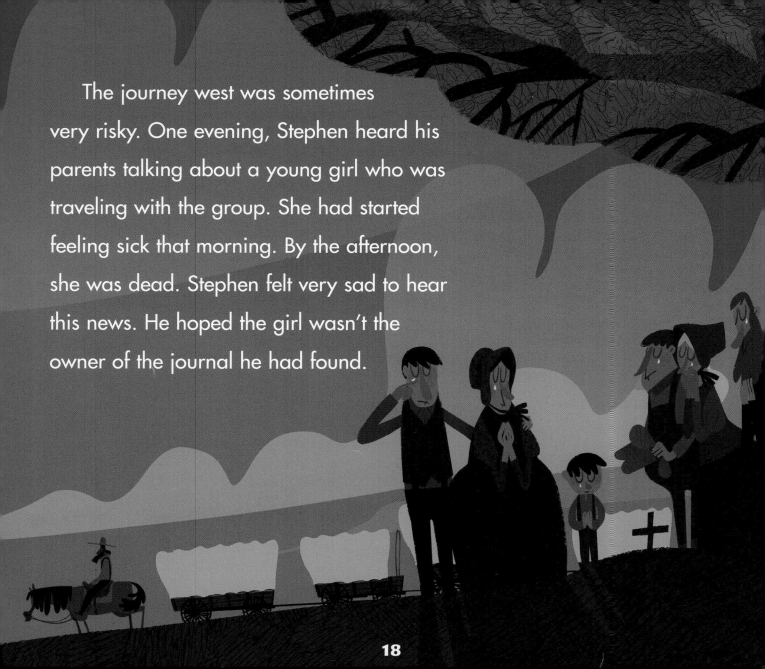

The journey west was sometimes
very risky. One evening, Stephen heard his
parents talking about a young girl who was
traveling with the group. She had started
feeling sick that morning. By the afternoon,
she was dead. Stephen felt very sad to hear
this news. He hoped the girl wasn't the
owner of the journal he had found.

TRAVELING WITHOUT DOCTORS OR MEDICINE

Many illnesses that are easily treated today were much more dangerous during the time of the Oregon Trail. A case of the flu or the measles could be deadly. People on the trail did not have access to doctors. They also didn't have the medicines we use today. **Cholera** and **smallpox** are serious diseases that can be cured now. But they were a risk for people traveling on the Oregon Trail.

The gravestone of a woman who died of cholera while traveling west in 1852

One night, as the group neared Oregon, there was a small celebration. Everyone was excited that the journey was almost over. Everyone talked, danced, and laughed around a big fire. Josephine spotted a boy sitting by himself.

"Hi!" she said with a smile as she walked toward him.

"I'm Josephine!"

"My name's Stephen," he replied, returning her smile.

TIME TO HAVE FUN

Along the trail, people had to find ways to entertain themselves. Some might have brought along musical instruments. Others might have sung songs or told stories around a campfire.

Settlers played instruments such as the violin.

Stephen and Josephine told each other why their families were moving to Oregon. They also talked about everything they had seen along the trail.

"I only wish I still had my journal," Josephine said. "I really wanted to write about last week when we met that group of native people."

A look of surprise crossed Stephen's face. He suddenly stood up and ran toward his family's wagon. Josephine watched with curiosity as he came back carrying a small object. It was her journal!

MEETING NATIVE PEOPLE

Oregon Trail travelers often met Native Americans during their journey west. Tribes such as the Shoshone, Sioux, and Ute were among the people who lived in the areas the trail crossed. Most meetings between the Native Americans and the settlers were peaceful. Sometimes they traded for food and other supplies.

Shoshone people near their homes in what is now Wyoming

Stephen and Josephine quickly became good friends. They talked often as they walked along the trail together. After a couple of weeks, they finally arrived in Oregon City. Josephine's family was staying in town, but the Byrds were traveling a little farther to reach their farmland. The two friends promised to stay in touch and visit when they could.

BRAND NEW HOMES

In the early days of the Oregon Trail, settlers did not arrive in fully developed towns and cities. There might be a town center with a handful of buildings. Some settlers would have set up campsites and farms nearby. As more people arrived, more buildings, streets, and other structures sprang up.

The city of Portland, Oregon, in 1853

In town, Josephine and her family finally joined her father. He was excited to show them the new house he had built. The family would surely be happy there now that they were together again.

Meanwhile, Stephen and his family arrived on their new land. They had a lot of work to do. However, they were thrilled to be starting their new lives in the West. It was November 1845, and Josephine and Stephen had a lifetime ahead of them.

A GROWING NATION

The Oregon Trail played a very important role in the growth of the United States. Hundreds of thousands of people traveled west along the trail. Around 40,000 of them were children.

Descendants of Oregon Trail settlers gather at the end of the trail in the early 1900s to celebrate their history.

OREGON CITY

OREGON

IDAHO

WYOMING

N

W   E

S

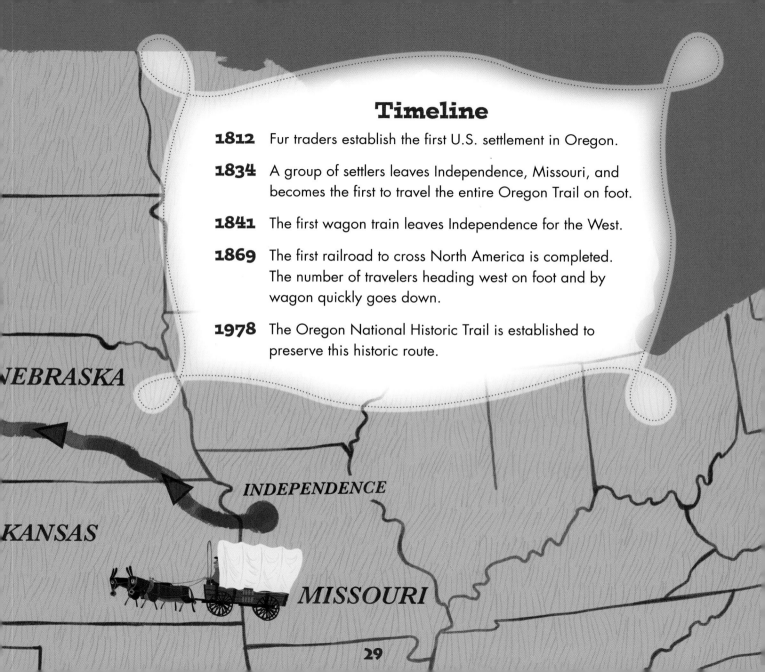

Timeline

1812 Fur traders establish the first U.S. settlement in Oregon.

1834 A group of settlers leaves Independence, Missouri, and becomes the first to travel the entire Oregon Trail on foot.

1841 The first wagon train leaves Independence for the West.

1869 The first railroad to cross North America is completed. The number of travelers heading west on foot and by wagon quickly goes down.

1978 The Oregon National Historic Trail is established to preserve this historic route.

NEBRASKA

INDEPENDENCE

KANSAS

MISSOURI

Words to Know

cholera (KAH-lur-uh) a dangerous disease that causes very bad vomiting and diarrhea, usually due to contaminated water

emigrants (EM-i-gruhnts) people who leave their homes to live in a new location

smallpox (SMAWL-poks) a very contagious disease that causes a rash, high fever, and blisters that can leave permanent scars

terrain (tuh-RAYN) an area of land

vast (VAST) very large in extent and amount

Index

ABOUT THE AUTHOR

Josh Gregory is the author of more than 90 books for kids. He has written about everything from animals to technology to history. A graduate of the University of Missouri–Columbia, he currently lives in Portland, Oregon.

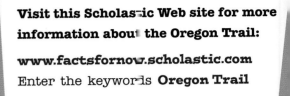

Visit this Scholastic Web site for more information about the Oregon Trail:

www.factsfornow.scholastic.com
Enter the keywords **Oregon Trail**

ABOUT THE ILLUSTRATOR

After illustrating more than 100 books over the past 20 years, Lluís Farré has drawn around 40 witches, 200 dragons, 500 princesses (and the corresponding princes), and more than 1,000 kids from different parts of the world and different moments in history. He lives far away from Oregon, in the coastal city of Barcelona, Spain.